AUSTRALIAN HOMESCHOOLING SERIES

T0363256

Test Your English 8

Years 8–10

CORONEOS PUBLICATIONS

Item No 566

This book is available from recognised booksellers or contact:

Coroneos Publications

Telephone: (02) 9838 9265   **Facsimile:** (02) 9838 8982
Business Address: 2/195 Prospect Highway Seven Hills 2147
Website: www.coroneos.com.au
E-mail: info@fivesenseseducation.com.au

Item # 566
Test Your English 8
by Valerie Marett
First published 2017

ISBN: 978-1-922034-75-5
© Valerie Marett

Test Your English 8

How to Use This Book

Score each page. Write the scores in the box. Mark as you go. You will find a checklist at the back of the book to use when correcting written expression exercises. Deduct one mark for each mistake in these exercises unless indicated.

Each section of the test indicates skills passed or failed. Answers are at the back of the book. <u>Complete one section at a time.</u> Your child may use a dictionary.

Do not help your child. <u>Do not proceed to the next section if your child has failed to gain the required score.</u>

Instructions on how to use the scores to discover which books are necessary to improve your child's knowledge are given on the next page.

Section 1

1	2	3	4	5	6	7	8	9
10	11	12	13	14	15	16	17	18
19	20	21	22	23	24	25	26	

Score: /545
Pass: 430/545

Section 2

1	2	3	4	5	6	7	8	9
10	11	12	13	14	15	16	17	18
19	20	21	22	23	24			

Score: /470
Pass: 369/470

To assess results go to page 2.

Section 1

401 or above: proceed to **Section 2** of the test.

276— 403   Work through *Successful English 7A*.

Below 275   Work through *Successful English 6A* and *6B* before proceeding further.

N.B. If grammar and/or written expression or both have been a major problem throughout this section you are best to go back to Successful English 6A and 6B to ensure the student has a solid foundation. Do not worry about the number on the book. Consider it a level. Rather worry about the student's knowledge of fundamentals they will need all their life.

Section 2

308 or above: Proceed to *Successful English 8A*.

246—308   Work through *Successful English 7B*.

Below 246:   While your child may have passed Section 1 of this test, it is suggested that you first work through *Successful English 7A and 7B*. **Note:** *Successful English 7A* is compulsory if the student is working towards a year 10 Certificate.

Note:
Do not worry about your child's grade levels. This series is a high standard. Knowledge is more important than grade levels.

If your child has passed this test but has large gaps in **either** grammar or written expression, it would be best to work from *Successful English 7A and 7B* before proceeding further. Each level of *Successful English* builds on knowledge learnt in previous levels.

Reading: If your child has had trouble reading this book, regardless of their grade, they should complete *Phonics Workbooks 1-4* The reading problem needs to be dealt with first. This is generally due to a lack of phonetical knowledge.

Section 1, Test 1: Nouns

A. List 4 examples of nouns that are neuter gender. (1 point each)

1. _____ 2. _____ 3. _____ 4. _____

B. Name 9 nouns and pronouns that are common gender. (1 point each)

_____

_____

C. Use a collective noun to complete each phrase below. (1 point each)

1. a _____ of directors   2. a _____ of savages

3. a _____ of kangaroos   4. a _____ of playing cards

5. a _____ of steps   6. a _____ of bees

D. Write the correct abstract noun to fit each definition below. (1 point each)

1. The state of being above average   _____

2. The state of being free from pretence or deceit   _____

3. The state of being on time   _____

4. The state of being willing to put up with pain, trouble,
    waiting etc.   _____

E. Write a noun listing a small quantity of something, e.g., a splinter of wood. (1 point each)

1. a _____ of dust   2. a _____ of grass

3. a _____ of glass   4. a _____ of bread

5. a _____ of rain   6. a _____ of hair

F. Rewrite the sentence, replacing the underlined part of the sentence with a noun. (1 point each)

My friend is a <u>person who always sees the worst side of life.</u>

_____

Score: /30   **Pass: 25/30**

Section 1, Test 2: Noun Plurals

Write the plural form of each noun listed below. (1 point each)

1. calf	_____	2. cherry	_____
3. volcano	_____	4. mumps	_____
5. mother-in-law	_____	6. antennae	_____
7. class	_____	8. terminus	_____
9. loaf	_____	10. victory	_____
11. handkerchief	_____	12. delay	_____
13. half	_____	14. louse	_____
15. patch	_____	16. legislation	_____
17. vertebra	_____	18. bacillus	_____
19. analysis	_____	20. criterion	_____
21. luggage	_____	22. passer-by	_____

B. Rewrite each sentence, changing the word in brackets to a plural.
(1 point each)

1. Please buy me six (tomato) while you are out.

_____

2. It has been bitterly cold and our area is experiencing a plague of (mouse).

_____

3. There are few (oasis) in the Nafud Desert.

_____

4. I have had several different (secretary) this year.

_____

5. There are many (pupa) in my garden waiting until spring to hatch.

_____

Score: /27   **Pass: 21/27**

© Valerie Marett
Coroneos Publications

Australian Homeschooling #566
Test Your English 8

Section 1, Test 3: Correct Meaning, Correct Ending

Many mistakes are made in English due to confusion arising from the similarity of sound or appearance of certain words.

A. Choose the correct word in brackets that means the same as the word or words in the first column. (1 point each)

1.	standing still	(stationery, stationary)	_____
2.	clever	(ingenious, ingenuous)	_____
3.	despicable	(contemptuous, contemptible)	_____
4.	to influence	(affect, effect)	_____
5.	bearing or appearance	(mean, mien)	_____

B. Complete each sentence below by adding "—ary" or "—ery". (1 point each)

1. Flatt_____ is only of second_____ importance.

2. In the Sahara Desert I found it necess_____ to ride a dromed_____ to the apothec_____ for some propriet_____ medicine.

C. Complete each sentence below by adding "—cy" or "—sy." ("—sy" is rare.)

1. In some countries you can be executed for here_____.

2. We'll begin our occupan____ of the house in December.

3. Sleeping in at the weekend is sheer ecsta_____.

D. Each sentence below contains the "—efy" or "—ify". Complete by adding "e" or "i" in the space indicated. (1 point each)

1. If Joel can't ver_____ his point, he will be mortified.

2. Unfrozen meat will soon putr_____.

E. Add "—ceed," "—cede" or "—sede" to the following to form complete words. (1 point each)

1. ac_____	2. super_____	3. ex_____
4. pro_____	5. re_____	6. suc_____

Score: /22   **Pass: 17/22**

© Valerie Marett
Coroneos Publications

Australian Homeschooling #566
Test Your English 8

Section 1, Test 4: Comprehension

Pax Romana, Latin for Roman Peace, refers to the Roman Empire in its prime. From the end of the Republican civil wars, beginning with the accession of Augustus in 27 BC, this era in Roman history lasted until 180 AD and the death of Marcus Aurelius. Prior to it there had never been peace for so many centuries in a given period of history. Pax Romana extended from Britain, Germany, down to Spain and then all round the Mediterranean to the top of Africa.

Since this area was so huge, everywhere Romans went they built roads, all leading back to Rome. These roads enabled the army to get from one end of the Empire to the other very quickly; imperial messengers carried orders; and trade flowed from the provinces to Rome. The Roman road system spanned more than 400,000 km of roads, including over 80,500 km of paved roads. When Rome reached the height of its power, no fewer than 29 great military highways radiated from the city. Hills were cut through and deep ravines filled in.

The Roman Army that marched along these roads were well trained and equipped. The legionary's clothing was well designed to protect the vital parts of his head and body without impeding his movements. His shield was designed to fit together with the shields of other soldiers to form a solid wall or "tortoise" covering over their heads. This prevented arrows from hitting them.

Each man had a pair of javelins. Hundreds of javelins would be thrown at once. These javelins were specially designed so that if they stuck in an enemy's shield they would bend or break when being pulled out, so they could not be hurled back at the Romans.

After the volley of javelins the Romans relied on their sword, a short thrusting sword, that was quicker and gave more dangerous wounds unlike the barbarians who had long, slashing swords. In addition they carried a dagger called a pugio. It had a very short but wide leaf type blade, about 170 to 270 cm long, which was used for stabbing and thrusting when fighting in close quarters with the enemy. When they were in close formation and the sword or spear could not be used, the Roman dagger was the next weapon of choice.

Along with the Army went engineers to plan camps and forts and design bridges and roads; doctors to cure the wounded; light troops on horses with slings or bows, artillery men with their catapults and carts with food supplies.

The Roman Army was taught to fight like a machine. Every man had his job and knew how important it was to keep his place in line with the right amount of space to use weapons, and how important it was to obey orders. Compared to the Roman Army many of the tribes the Romans fought in the west seemed a mob, every man fighting for himself. Finally, when they had won, the Romans built forts to watch the new frontier and roads to join the forts together. They were built in such a way that they gave soldiers quick access to the walls.

Answer these questions:

1. How long did the period of Roman Peace last? (2 points)

   _____

2. How far did the Roman Empire extend during this period? (2 points)

   _____

   _____

3. Name the two things that Rome did as soon as it established new territory. (1 point)_____

4. What was the main purpose of the roads? (2 points)

   _____

   _____

5. Think! What was the other benefit to the citizens of the Empire? (1 point)

   _____

6. List the legionary's clothing and equipment and its purpose.(5 points)

   _____

   _____

   _____

7. Who else travelled with the army? (2 points)

   _____

   _____

8. Was the Roman Army well trained? Explain your answer. (2 points)

   _____

   _____

B. Word Knowledge: find words in the text that fit the following definition: (1 point)

1. a short dagger used for thrusting and stabbing
   in close quarters   _____

2. preventing or hindering   _____

3. Roman peace   _____

4. spears all discharged at once   _____

Score: /21   **Pass: 18/21**

Section 1, Test 5: Verbs

A. Identify the verb in each sentence below and write the verb and state its type, e.g., finite, transitive, infinitive, participles etc. (1 point each verb, 1 point each type, 12 points total)

1. Mr Jones finished his work and went home.

    _____

2. The mother quietly instructed her children on their tasks.

    _____

3. David is swimming well today.

    _____

4. The girl shouted at the top of her lungs.

    _____

B. Identify the noun or nouns and verb or verbs in each sentence below. Write them on the line provided. (You may count pronouns as nouns for this exercise.) (1 point each, 33 points total)

1. Dad was paddling my canoe in the Father's Day race.

    _____

2. The clown tumbled gaily into the ring as the spectators screamed with delight.

    _____

3. The schooner did not put out to sea while the wild storm was raging.

    _____

4. If you do this work well I will let you go swimming.

    _____

5. He roams alone where the wild dogs go.

    _____

6. Recently he met Dawn Fraser, who swam in the Olympics many years ago.

    _____

Score: /45   **Pass: 35/45**

Section 1, Test 6: French Words & Phrases Used Commonly

English contains many words of French origin that have become Anglicised over the years, e.g., machine, force, police, routine.

Match the definition to the correct word or phrase in the box. (1 point each)

> resume; tete-a-tete; nom de plume; boutique; a la carte;
> fait accompli; repertoire; au fait; debut; vinaigrette; façade;
> a la mode; sabotage; premiere; bon appetit

1. a body of items regularly performed   _____

2. fashionable   _____

3. first performance of a play or film   _____

4. individual dish ordered rather than a fixed meal _____

5. a fake persona   _____

6. an intimate get together or private conversation
    between two people   _____

7. good appetite; enjoy your food   _____

8. first public performance of an entertainment
    personality or group   _____

9. author's pseudonym   _____

10. salad dressing of oil and vinegar   _____

11. a document listing one's qualifications for a job _____

12. being conversant in or instructed in or with   _____

13. subversive destruction   _____

14. an accomplished fact; something that has
    already happened and is unlikely to be repeated _____

15. a clothing store usually selling designer clothes
    rather than mass produced ones   _____

Score: /15   **Pass: 12/15**

Section 1, Test 7: Adjectives

A. Look at each sentence below. Say which class each of the underlined adjectives belongs. State the noun it qualifies.

1. **Which** article did you write in the magazine? (2 points)

_____

2. The **third** applicant was **my** brother who was highly qualified. (4 points)

_____

3. **Every** test must be given to **those** pupils sitting **this** exam. (6 points)

_____

4. A **huge** rock rolled down the **steep** hill gathering more rocks in the process.
(4 points)_____

B. Rewrite the sentences below, substituting a single adjective from the box for each underlined phrase. Be careful, you may need to rearrange the sentence.
For example: We noticed several houses **in which nobody lives.**
We noticed several uninhabited houses. (1 point each)

insurmountable, unceremonious, impenetrable, unprecedented, aquatic

1. The jungle proved **too dense to be penetrated.**

_____

2. This is the first time the event **taking place on the water** has been performed.

_____

3. The early settlers saw the Great Dividing Range as a barrier **that could not be crossed.**

_____

4. It was an event **for which there was no previous example.**

_____

5. The visitor behaved in a manner **that was informal and rather abrupt, even a little discourteous.**

_____

Score: /21

Pass: 17/21

Australian Homeschooling #566
Test Your English 8

Section 1, Test 8: Figures of Speech

Say if the following figures of speech are similes, metaphors, puns, hyperbole, onomatopoeia, personification or alliteration. (1 point each)

1.	The ocean danced in the moonlight.	_____
2.	Tim took tons of tools to make toys for tots.	_____
3.	I can smell food from a mile away.	_____
4.	The teacher planted seeds of wisdom in his mind.	_____
5.	John was as blind as a bat.	_____
6.	Sign at a deer crossing: the buck stops here.	_____
7.	Bring… Bring… The alarm clock clanged in the dark and silent room.	_____
8.	My mother is going to kill me.	_____

Similes

B. Similes are common figures of everyday speech. Put each simile below into a sentence. Write a complex sentence and don't just add two or three words. (2 points each)

1. as white as snow: _____

    _____

2. as cold as ice: _____

    _____

3. to eat like a horse: _____

    _____

C. Explain the following similes. (1 point each)

1. to sleep like a log: _____

2. as sharp as a knife: _____

3. to work like a dog: _____

Score: /17   **Pass: 12/17**

© Valerie Marett
Coroneos Publications

Australian Homeschooling #566
Test Your English 8

Section 1, Test 9: Adverbs

A. Look at each sentence. State whether the adverb in bold in each sentence modifies a verb, an adjective or an adverb. (1 point each)

1. The woman is **very** pretty. _____

2. The girl crept **silently** down the stairs. _____

3. The paintings are kept in a **dimly** lit room. _____

4. He runs **really** quickly. _____

5. You may use your laptop in class **tomorrow**. _____

6. The idea is **simply** ridiculous. _____

7. She served **slightly** better this game than last game. _____

8. John **easily** lifted the crate. _____

B. Underline the adverb and state whether it is an adverb of manner, time or place. (2 points each sentence)

1. We'll meet again next week. _____

2. I left the book here while I had dinner. _____

3. John ate his pear nosily and Mum was not pleased with his manners.
_____

4. Dad drove slowly over the bridge looking for the exit to the town.
_____

5. The children can play outside while we talk. _____

6. I intend to buy a new computer tomorrow. _____

7. Please do it now David and do not argue with me.
_____

8. Listen to me carefully. _____

9. Dad will come here to get us. _____

Score: /26   Pass: 21/26

© Valerie Marett
Coroneos Publications

Australian Homeschooling #566
Test Your English 8

Section 1, Test 10: French Words & Phrases Used in English.

Match the definition to the correct word or phrase in the box. (1 point each)

café au lait, maître d', faux pas, protégé, par excellence, attaché
haute coutre, piece de resistance, en route, cordon bleu, au fait,
en suite, hors d'oeuvre, potpourri, petit four, matinee, déjà vu

1. small dessert, especially a cake _____

2. conversant with, informed _____

3. an outstanding accomplishment or the final part
   of something, e.g., a project, meal etc. _____

4. someone who is trained or sponsored by an
   influential person _____

5. a feeling like you have that you have already seen or
   done something when you are sure you haven't _____

6. person assigned to a diplomatic post _____

7. an appetizer before the main meal _____

8. high class, expensive clothing style _____

9. coffee with milk _____

10. a foolish mistake, something that shouldn't be done _____

11. pre-eminent, the best of the best _____

12. "blue ribbon," Master Chef _____

13. master of the dining room _____

14. on the way _____

15. part of a set, together, often used to refer to a small
    bathroom joined onto a bedroom _____

16. the day's first showing of a movie or play _____

17. scented mixture of dried flowers and spice _____

Score: /17   **Pass: 13/17**

Section 1, Test 11: Common Figurative Expressions

Choose a figurative expression from the box at the bottom to fit each meaning. Write it on the line. (1 point each)

1. to join the party that seems to be winning _____

2. to avoid being friendly with someone _____

3. to put an end to something _____

4. to extract and make use of another person's ideas _____

5. a mess or a muddle _____

6. to handle a situation in an impromptu manner _____

7. to be caught doing something wrong with evidence there for all to see _____

8. to state a fact that allows no doubt _____

9. a feeling of unpleasant distaste _____

10. take a subordinate position _____

11. an unauthorised court, rough justice _____

12. a deliberate provocation, sure to have an adverse reaction _____

13. to be alert, in command of one's senses _____

14. act submissively and apologetically, especially in admitting one's error _____

---

to ring down the curtain
to climb on the bandwagon
caught red-handed
to keep someone at arm's length
to set one's teeth on edge
a dog's breakfast
eat humble pie

make no bones about it
to play it by ear
take a back seat
to pick someone's brains
a kangaroo court
on the ball
a red rag to a bull

Score: /14

Pass: 11/14

© Valerie Marett
Coroneos Publications

Australian Homeschooling #566
Test Your English 8

Section 1, Test 12: Pronouns

There are nine main classes of pronouns: personal, impersonal, relative, interrogative, reflexive, possessive, distributive, demonstrative, and indefinite. For each sentence, on the space provided write the pronoun and say what class it is. (2 points each question)

1. If little is expected, little will be achieved. _____

2. Mary and I deceived ourselves into believing that money given us was free. _____

3. My mother and I each had a cake. _____

4. Those pancakes were even better than yesterday's. _____

5. Look at those girl's dresses. Theirs are even better than ours. _____

6. Everyone here earns more than a thousand dollars a week. _____

7. If he parks his car without putting a coin in the meter he will be fined. _____

8. She injured herself playing basketball. _____

9. What did he say to you just now? _____

10. The new, white car is mine. _____

11. There's something in my shoe. _____

12. It is Monday today. _____

13. This parcel was sent from overseas. _____

14. I saw a little girl who was very beautiful. _____

15. Either road will take you to the shopping centre. _____

16. Some are born great; some achieve greatness. _____

Score: /32   Pass: 26/32

Section 1, Test 13: Inserting Proper Nouns

Insert the proper noun from the box into the correct space below. Use ach only once. (1 point each)

> Mississippi, Virgin, Mandarin, Holden, Montreal, Victoria, Tasmania, China, Mars, Endeavour, Marie, Pacific, Francis Drake, Christmas, Governor General January, Uluru, Mozart, Alexander Bell, Kosciusko, South America, Robert Scott,

1. country _____

2. month _____

3. city _____

4. ocean _____

5. inventor _____

6. airline _____

7. planet _____

8. explorer _____

9. admiral _____

10. car _____

11. ship _____

12. river _____

13. island _____

14. composer _____

15. mountain _____

16. language _____

17. holiday _____

18. title _____

19. state _____

20. girl _____

21. rock _____

22. continent _____

Food Twins

Complete the following by matching the food with a word from the box.
(1 point each)

> eggs, crackers, cream, tomato sauce, lemons, marmalade, chips, mint sauce

1. fish and _____

2. apple pie and _____

3. meat pie and _____

4. lamb and _____

5. cheese and _____

6. oranges and _____

7. bacon and _____

8. toast and _____

Score: /30

Pass: 24/30

© Valerie Marett
Coroneos Publications

Australian Homeschooling #566
Test Your English 8

Section 1, Test 14: Prepositions

A. **Look at each sentence below. Study each underlined preposition. State:**
- **what noun or noun equivalent it governs**
- **what phrase it introduces**
- **between what two words it shows the relationship.**

1. The jug, which was fortunately empty, hit him on the head. (4 points)

   _____

2. His eyes fell on the flag flapping in the breeze. (8 points)

   _____

   _____

3. Mr Jones passed the salt to his friend. (4 points)

   _____

4. The girl with the red skirt looks upset.   (4 points)

   _____

B. Insert the correct preposition in the following sentences. (1 point each space)

1. I shall appeal _____ the directors _____ this unfair decision.

2. I want to impress _____ you the importance of being on time for this appointment. It is a very busy day.

3. May I come in? I do not want to intrude _____ you if you are busy.

4. Just leave me the salad and divide the rest of the food _____ the three of you.

5. The numbers on this docket correspond _____ the numbers on this package.

6. John wished to confer _____ his father on the price before he bought the house.

7. The Council meeting was in an uproar as some councillors argued

   _____ the proposal and some _____ it.

8. The soldier was invested _____ the highest honour a nation could bestow, the Victoria Cross.

Score: /30   **Pass: 26/30**

Section 1, Test 15: Ambiguity

It is important to write correctly so there is no ambiguity. Ambiguity is doubt or uncertainty regarding what the writer intended. Rewrite the following sentences so the meaning becomes clear. (2 points each sentence.)

1. This the room with the strange keyhole in which Lord Byron was born.

   _____

2. I have a picture of the place in my mind where we saw all that rubbish.

   _____

3. To Rent: Neat, well-kept townhouse with two bedrooms and spacious bathroom, at present occupied by the owner.

   _____

   _____

4. Climbing a hill, a creek flowed below them.

   _____

5. She was surprised by Mr Stephens putting on lipstick.

   _____

6. The farmer wanted a man to look after the cow who could keep his accounts.

   _____

   _____

7. He was run over by a car skipping down the hill.

   _____

8. We have all read your book and many like it.

   _____

9. He watched the approach of the storm sitting in the car.

   _____

10. We found the dog belonging to the lady called Spot.

   _____

Score: /20   **Pass: 16/20**

Section 1, Test 16: Conjunctions

A. A conjunction joins two single words, two phrases or two clauses. Rewrite each sentence using the conjunction in the box to complete the sentences below. You may use each conjunction only once. (1 point each sentence)

that	and	as	though	even though	or

1. Shall we go swimming? Shall we play tennis?

   _____

2. Ian won the race. He was not considered a good runner.

   _____

3. He is not sure. He will be able to come.

   _____

4. I looked for it. John would not help me.

   _____

5. He opened his book. He read a chapter.

   _____

6. We held the oars. We had been instructed.

   _____

B. Underline the conjunction in each sentence below. (1 point each)

1. Wherever he went, bad luck dogged his footsteps.

2. We need to stocktake in order to know what our stock level is for tax purposes.

3. People shudder whenever they see the remnants of the wrecked plane.

4. So that we should not miss him, he wore a red buttonhole.

5. I think this is the man although I have not seen him before.

C. Complete each sentence with a suitable conjunction: (1 point each)

1. A boy emerged from the house _____ looked across at me.

2. _____ was now dark they decided to end the search.

Score: /13   Pass: 10/13

Section 1, Test 17: Sentences

There are 4 main types of sentences: statements, questions, commands and exclamations. In addition there are greetings and responses. These can all be broken down into further groups.

Identify each type of sentence. Make sure your answer is complete, e.g., What is the capital of Peru? This a question seeking to elicit a direct answer. **There are fourteen groups. 11 are used below. Use each only once.** (2 points each)

1. Eat your sandwich before you leave the table.

    _____

2. Good morning, Joel.

    _____

3. Things will probably all go wrong on the day.

    _____

4. Does anyone like that politician?

    _____

5. Yes, I see.

    _____

6. You are welcome.

    _____

7. It looks as though it will be a nice day.

    _____

8. Did you brush your teeth before getting into bed?

    _____

9. Just a moment.

    _____

10. Should I spend the money?

    _____

11. It's just not right.

    _____

Score: /22   **Pass: 16/22**

Section 1, Test 18: Choosing the Right Word

A word is missing from each of the following sentences. In each case choose the correct word from the word in the brackets. (1 point)

1. The manager thought the new employee's attitude to his job was too
   _____. (casual, causal)

2. His story was _____ by other evidence which made it more convincing. (collaborated, corroborated)

3. A clear policy _____ from the Cabinet meeting.
   (eventuated, happened, transpired)

4. The family had to be _____ in their use of money if they wished to feed their large family. (economic, economical)

5. The advertisement announcing the vacancy specifically _____ those without degrees. (eliminated, excluded)

6. The country house with its trees was an _____ of peace. (idle, idol, idyll)

7. The Government's anti-inflation policy was a _____ factor in the high unemployment rate. (casual, causal)

8. You can go there by bus or by train, but most people prefer the _____. (last, later, latter)

9. The court found the newspaper guilty of _____ and awarded substantial damages to the plaintiff. (libel, slander)

10. That site will be the ideal _____ for the cricket ground. (locality, location)

11. The champion golfer gave a _____ performance. (masterful, masterly)

12. He was _____ to leave a place where he had enjoyed himself so much. (loathe, loath, loth)

13. He was so absorbed in his music he was _____ of his surroundings. (oblivious, ignorant of)

14. There was much civil strife over the _____ of the weak king. (rain, reign, rein)

Score: /14   **Pass: 11/14**

© Valerie Marett
Coroneos Publications

Australian Homeschooling #566
Test Your English 8

Section 1, Test 19: Important Definitions

Look at each example below. Decide which of the following terms best fits and write it in the space provided: alliteration, anticlimax, antithesis, cliché, couplet, epigram, epitaph, fable, irony, spoonerism. (1 point each)

1. A dog stole a joint of meat and ran away with it across a bridge. As he looked in the water he thought he saw another dog with a joint of meat. He opened his jaws to seize the other joint, and so lost what he had.

   _____

2. She happily helped the homeless.

   _____

3. I went to school to study to be anything but a painter and now I am a painter.

   _____

4. Because I waddle when I walk,
   Should this give rise to silly talk.   (The Dachshund by Edward Anthony)

   _____

5. Death is a debt to nature which I have paid and so must you.

   _____

6. People in glass houses shouldn't throw stones.

   _____

7. thick as thieves

   _____

8. I went on holiday with my Mum, my Dad, my sister and my camera.

   _____

9. A lack of pies. (A pack of lies.)

   _____

10. She was easy on the eye but hard on the heart.

    _____

Score: /10   **Pass: 8/10**

© Valerie Marett
Coroneos Publications

Australian Homeschooling #566
Test Your English 8

Section 1, Test 20: Subject, Predicate, Object

Look at each sentence. Decide which is the subject, predicate and object. Write them in the box provided lower down the page. Underline the verb. Be careful! Find the simple sentence first.

1. She drank a bottle of water. (2 points)

2. Oxygen is essential for life on earth. (2 points)

3. Children who behave badly create problems. (4 points)

4. His sister mended them with great skill. (2 points)

5. Be careful! That dog will bite your hand! (4 points)

6. We ate a hamburger at Hungry Jack's. (2 points)

7. Dad bought his son a new coat. (3 points)

8. Everyone brought food today. (2 points)

9. Roger lent Stephen his camera (3 points)

10. We saw and touched the baby koala. (2 points)

Subject	Predicate	Object

Score: /26   Pass: 19/26

Section 1, Test 21:Malapropisms

Each of the sentences below contains a malapropism, which is shown in bold. Replace it with the correct word from the box. (1 point each space)

> endure, amphibious, contiguous, inexperience, monogamy, infuriated, inured, incandescent, auspicious, credible, bracing, equivocal, geography, electrocutions, vociferous, emetics

1. Some of the adventures he claimed to have had were so strange they were hardly **creditable** _____.

2. Dr Brown administered **cosmetics** _____ to induce vomiting.

3. The man's **equivalent** _____ replies to their questions aroused the suspicion of the police.

4. In some countries if the first baby is a boy it is considered a **suspicious** _____ event.

5. The air in Tasmania is very **embracing** _____ in winter.

6. Since it can live on both land and water a frog is described as **ambiguous** _____.

7. In this country a man can have only one wife. This is called **monotony** _____.

8. I wanted my daughter instructed in **geometry** _____ so she would know something about **contagious** _____ countries.

9. Mary was **infused** _____ by a driver who nearly collided with her.

10. He was **invalidated** _____ to the comments made about his red hair.

11. The laying of the roof bats led to several **elocutions** _____ due to the **inexpedience** _____ of some workers.

12. Most politicians must **endear** _____ a great many **voracious** _____ interruptions at public meetings.

Score: /15　　　　　　　　　　　　　　**Pass: 11/15**

Section 1, Test 22: Main and Subordinate Clauses

Look at each sentence below. Identify the main clause and subordinate clause and write them in the appropriate place. (2 points per question)

1. Gordon forgot his sunscreen even though he knew he burnt easily.

Main clause: _____

Subordinate clause: _____

2. When the airplane landed, the engine was smoking.

Main clause: _____

Subordinate clause: _____

3. Max went shopping for books and bought some that were on sale.

Main clause: _____

Subordinate clause: _____

4. After John caught the fish, Kelly caught one also.

Main clause: _____

Subordinate clause: _____

5. I like to eat lunch outside when the sun is shining.

Main clause: _____

Subordinate clause: _____

6. The ball bounced onto the roof where Casey and Robert can not reach it.

Main clause: _____

Subordinate clause: _____

7. Although Tom plays many sports, he likes playing tennis best.

Main clause: _____

Subordinate clause: _____

Score: /14   **Pass: 11/14**

© Valerie Marett
Coroneos Publications

Australian Homeschooling #566
Test Your English 8

Section 1, Test 23: Using One Word for Many

Rewrite the sentences below, substituting a single word for the words that are underlined. Choose from the words in the box. (1 point each sentence.)

> prescribed, infallible, ambidextrous, conspicuous, procrastination, irresponsibly, pessimists, ubiquitous, rhetoric, exonerate

1. He acted <u>in a way that showed he had no sense of responsibility.</u>

   _____

2. The judge could not <u>free</u> the accused <u>from all blame for what had happened.</u>

   _____

3. At last he was able to convince <u>all the people who thought the worst would happen</u> that there was still hope.

   _____

4. Lost on their hike, the scouts no longer regarded their patrol leader as <u>one who can not err.</u>

   _____

5. Rabbits were at one time <u>to be found everywhere</u> in Australia.

   _____

6. My brother is <u>able to use either hand with ease.</u>

   _____

7. The company <u>layed down as a rule</u> fixed hours for its employees.

   _____

8. The accident left him with <u>a clearly visible</u> scar on his face.

   _____

9. <u>The art of speaking to persuade</u> is often used unscrupulously.

   _____

10. <u>Putting off until later</u> is the thief of time.

   _____

Score: /10

Pass: 7/10

© Valerie Marett
Coroneos Publications

Australian Homeschooling #566
Test Your English 8

Section 1, Test 24: Words Using Latin Prefixes

Often one word can effectively replace several. Choose a Latin prefix from the box to fit each meaning. (1 point each question)

> unanimous, exculpate, subvert, redound, procrastinate, supersede, benevolent, interpose, posthumous, unison, preposterous, conjunction, recapitulate, disinter, recant, procure

1. born after death of its father _____

2. to give up an opinion or belief _____

3. repeat in outline; to go through the main points of a subject again _____

4. the act of overthrowing existing beliefs _____

5. unity of pitch of musical notes; agreement _____

6. to come back on a person _____

7. intended for doing good rather than making profit _____

8. the meeting of two or more planets when their longitudes are the same _____

9. to exhume; to unearth _____

10. to clear of guilt or blame _____

11. to insert or introduce between parts; to place oneself between others or a thing _____

12. contrary to reason or common sense; utterly absurd _____

13. to put off doing something, especially out of carelessness or laziness _____

14. to take the place or move into the position of _____

15. sharing the same opinion or views; in complete accord _____

16. to get by special effort; to obtain _____

Score: /16　　　　　　　　　　　　　**Pass: 12/16**

© Valerie Marett
Coroneos Publications

Australian Homeschooling #566
Test Your English 8

Section 1, Test 25: Figures of Speech and Poetic Devices

A. Rewrite each sentence changing the similes into metaphors. (2 points each)

1. Geology means no more to me than a closed book.

_____

2. You must tackle your difficulties resolutely, just as you would take a bull by the horns.

_____

3. You have things the wrong way round, just as though you were putting the cart before the horse.

_____

B. State whether each sentence contains personification, hyperbole, pun, epigram, onomatopoeia, alliteration, metaphor or simile. (1 point each)

1. A notice in a chemist window: we dispense with accuracy.   _____

2. Now air is hush'd, save when the weak eyed bat With short, shrill shriek flits by on leather wings.   _____

3. He snapped my head off.   _____

4. He did fly on the wings of the wind.   _____

5. Fortune can take from us nothing but what she gave us.   _____

6. The only thing that experience teaches us is that experience teaches us nothing.   _____

7. Over the cobbles he clattered and clashed   _____

8. She was leaning on a staff, the top of which was like the head of an eagle.   _____

9. Land of Hope and Glory, Mother of the Free   _____

10. It cracked and growled, and roared and howled   _____

Score: /16   **Pass: 13/16**

© Valerie Marett
Coroneos Publications

Australian Homeschooling #566
Test Your English 8

Section 1, Test 26: Adjectival Clauses

A. **Read the sentence. Write the adjectival clause in the space provided. Circle the noun or pronoun it modifies.** (2 points each)

1. How is your friend for whom I made this cake?

   _____

2. The group selected the student who wrote the best class song.

   _____

3. What is that you bought?

   _____

4. Olivia and Krystal had important duties which they handled very well.

   _____

5. Lisa is the customer who called this morning.

   _____

B. Underline the adjectival clause. Write the main clause on the line provided. (2 points each sentence)

1. Tell me about the place which you are moving to.

   _____

2. He is an author whose name is well known.

   _____

3. The man whom they named is a noted explorer.

   _____

4. Henry Parkes was one of those men who advocated the union of the Australian colonies.

   _____

5. There are few lands that he has not travelled.

   _____

6. Tell me about the place where you are going.

   _____

Score: /22   Pass: **18/22**

Section 2

Before proceeding to Section 2, score and add up tests 1-26. If your child has not scored 430 or above do not proceed to Section 2.

Section 2, Test 1: Better Words

A. Sometimes it is better to use one word. Look at the words in the box. Choose one word to replace those that are underlined. Rewrite the sentence. (1 point)

> speculation, jury, pessimist, junction, magnanimity, testimonial

1. The king showed <u>great noble-mindedness and generosity</u> in dealing with the rebels.

   _____

2. <u>The collection of people who had to decide the truth of the case being tried before the judge</u> found it difficult to come to a decision.

   _____

3. The train approached the <u>place where two lines meet.</u>

   _____

4. Who would win the Grand Final this year was a subject <u>for making guesses.</u>

   _____

5. My friend is a <u>person who always sees the worst side of life.</u>

   _____

B. Rewrite each sentence replacing each underlined word with a synonym from the box. (1 point each word)

> understanding, catastrophe, attempt, authentic, obstinate, ultimately, disorder, forged, incredible, remedy, attain

1. <u>Eventually</u>, if they persevere, they will <u>achieve</u> their aim.

   _____

2. The <u>disarray</u> of the room after the <u>disaster</u> was <u>almost unbelievable</u>.

   _____

3. A <u>genuine</u> masterpiece can easily be distinguished from a <u>fake</u> one.

   _____

4. His lack of <u>comprehension</u> was matched by his <u>stubborn</u> refusal to <u>endeavour</u> to <u>rectify</u> his weakness.

   _____

Score: /16   **Pass: 13/16**

© Valerie Marett
Coroneos Publications

Australian Homeschooling #566
Test Your English 8

Section 2, Test 2: Principal & Subordinate Clause

A. Find the principal and the subordinate clause in each sentence and write them in the lines provided. (1 point each part)

1. All the books which sounded very interesting have already been borrowed.

   Principal clause: _____

   Subordinate clause: _____

2. I am looking forward to the moment when I finish this course.

   Principal clause: _____

   Subordinate clause: _____

3. There is a man at the door who wants to see you.

   Principal clause: _____

   Subordinate clause: _____

4. Do you remember the name of the man whom you met yesterday?

   Principal clause: _____

   Subordinate clause: _____

5. The man, whose wife teaches English, is a professional tennis player.

   Principal clause: _____

   Subordinate clause: _____

6. Can you remember the exact spot you dropped it?

   Principal clause: _____

   Subordinate clause: _____

7. It is an ill wind that blows nobody any good.

   Principal clause: _____

   Subordinate clause: _____

8. None of those people whom he mentioned were known to us.

   Principal clause: _____

   Subordinate clause: _____

Score: /16   **Pass: 12/16**

© Valerie Marett
Coroneos Publications

Australian Homeschooling #566
Test Your English 8

Section 2, Test 3: Correct Usage

A. A verb agrees with its subject in person and number. Rewrite the sentences below choosing the correct verb from those in the brackets. (1 point each)

1. Hunger and thirst (is, are) the cause of much human suffering.

   _____

2. Surely each of these men (have been told, has been told) to come prepared for this trial.

   _____

   _____

3. Australia in cultivating and harvesting (is, are) highly mechanised.

   _____

4. Every one of the boys (has, have) finished their homework.

   _____

B. Correct the sentences below by replacing the wrong words in each sentence with the correct word or words in the list under the sentence.

1. It was I who you saw near the gate in the lane.
       a. me   b. which   c. whom   d. seen   (1 point)

   _____

2. Who's overnight bag was stuck by the hedge?
       a. beside   b. below   c. whos'   d. whose (2 points)

   _____

3. Jane said that her and me were the best cooks in the class.
       a. better   b. us   c. she and I   d. she   (1 point)

   _____

4. Always buy Cadbury's chocolate as they are the best on the market.
       a. better   b. it is   c. at   d. purchase   (1 point)

   _____

5. We weren't surprised at the result, but now he and I must prepare a new plan.
       a. were not   b. is   c. am   d. we   (2 points)

   _____

Score: /11   **Pass: 8/11**

Section 2, Test 4: Poetry

Colour

The lovely things that I have watched unthinking,
Unknowing, day by day,
That their soft dyes have steeped my soul in colour
That will not pass away -

Great saffron sunset clouds, and larkspur mountains,
And fenceless miles of plain,
And hillsides golden-green in that unearthly
Clear shining after rain;

And nights of blue and pearl, and long smooth beaches,
Yellow as sunburnt wheat,
Edged with a line of foam that creams and hisses,
Enticing weary feet.

And emeralds, and sunset-hearted opals,
And Asian marble, veined
With scarlet flame, and cool green jade, and moonstones
Misty and azure-stained;

And almond trees in bloom, and oleanders,
Or a wide purple sea,
Of plain-land gorgeous with a lovely poison,
The evil Darling pea.

If I am tired I call on these to help me
To dream -and dawn-lit skies,
Lemon and pink, or faintest, coolest lilac,
Float on my soothed eyes.

There is no night so black but you shine through it,
There is no morn so drear,
O Colour of the World, but I can find you,
Most tender, pure and clear.

Thanks be to God, Who gave this gift of colour,
Which who shall seek shall find;
Thanks be to God, Who gives me strength to hold it,
Though I were stricken blind.

by Dorothea McKellar

An Australian poet, Dorethea McKellar wrote the poem in 1909. It is one of her favourite poems.

A. Answer these questions:

1. What is the theme of the poem? (2 points)

   _____

   _____

2. Explain the form of the poem. (2 points)

   _____

   _____

3. Explain how the author has used contrasting colours in different verses to emphasise the range and beauty of the scenes around her. Give examples. (5 points)

   _____

   _____

   _____

   _____

4. The author has mostly used adjectives to emphasise the colours but the poem contains one metaphor, one simile and on example of onomatopoeia Write them below. (3 points)

   _____

   _____

   _____

5. In verse five the author speaks of "the evil Darling pea." What is she describing? Why is it evil? (2 point)

   _____

   _____

6. How has diction (word choice) influenced this poem? (3 points)

   _____

   _____

   _____

7. Read the first and last verse. Describe the author's main thought. (2 pt)

   _____

   _____

Score: /19   Pass: 15/19

Section 2, Test 5: Adjectival Clauses & Phrases

A. **Underline the <u>adjectival clause</u> in each of the following sentences. Circle the noun it modifies or relates to.** (2 points each question)

1. The station where we will leave the train is called Hopper Crossing.

2. I look forward to the moment when I finish work.

3. Do you know John whose daughter is going to marry Tony?

4. There is a man at the door who wants to see you.

5. Peter, who called a few minutes ago, wanted to know if you were coming tonight.

6. All the books which sounded interesting had already been borrowed.

B. Underline the <u>adjectival phrase</u> in each of the following sentences. Circle the noun it modifies or relates to. Be careful. There may be more than one.
(2 points each question)

1. Andrew, although a clever boy, never did well in exams.

2. The baby in the cot looked very sweet.

3. A calf near its mother ran away startled by the backfire of the car.

4. The book on the table contained many beautiful pictures.

Score: /20

Pass: 16/20

© Valerie Marett
Coroneos Publications

Australian Homeschooling #566
Test Your English 8

Section 2, Test 6: Word Usage

A. Complete the collective nouns. (1 point each)

1. a _____ of mountains
2. a _____ of paper
3. a _____ of tourists
4. a _____ of horsemen
5. an _____ of musicians
6. a _____ of magistrates
7. a _____ of oysters
8. a _____ of wombats
9. a _____ of cheetahs
10. a _____ of pups
11. a _____ of seagulls
12. a _____ of robbers

B. Write the plural form of the following words: (1 point each)

1. inferno _____
2. ratio _____
3. sheep _____
4. storey _____
5. memorandum _____
6. diagnosis _____
7. city _____
8. dingo _____
9. half _____
10. knife _____
11. species _____
12. wharf _____
13. bureau _____
14. criterion _____

C. Many mistakes come from the similarity in sound or appearance of certain words. Select one of the two words in brackets to fit the definition. (1 point each)

1. easy to read   (eligible, legible)   _____
2. reference   (allusion, illusion)   _____
3. enhance   (compliment, complement)   _____
4. despicable   (abhorrent, aberrant)   _____
5. to go ahead of   (precede, proceed)   _____
6. clever   (ingenious, ingenuous)   _____

Score: /32   Pass: 26/32

© Valerie Marett
Coroneos Publications

Australian Homeschooling #566
Test Your English 8

Section 2, Test 7: Adverbial Phrases & Clauses

A. Look at each sentence below. Underline the <u>adverbial phrase</u>. On the line provided say whether it tells how, when, where or why and the verb it modifies. Make sure you don't miss any. (3 points each question)

1. My brother shaves in the morning. _____

2. His sister mended the tear with great skill. _____

3. Underneath the old bucket we found a large brown snake.

   _____

4. In spite of the rain we enjoyed ourselves immensely.

   _____

5. William ran back inside the house for his raincoat.

   _____   _____

B. Write the <u>adverbial clause</u> on the line provided and say whether it is a clause of manner, time, place or reason and the verb it modifies. Make sure you don't miss any. (3 points each question)

1. The match was not played yesterday as it was too wet.

   _____

2. The boy shivered when the cold water sprayed him.

   _____

3. We practised writing the letters as our teacher had shown us.

   _____

4. We planted the tree where the hole had already been dug.

   _____

5. As his leg hurt he did not hurry after them.

   _____

6. To avoid being hurt I jumped into the ditch when I saw the cyclist.

   _____

7. Turn the handle to the right as the diagram shows.

Score: /36   **Pass: 30/36**

Section 2, Test 8: Correct Sentences

Rewrite and correct the following sentences. (2 points each sentence.)

1. Mr Jones finishes his work and goes home.

    _____

2. Dumb with astonishment, he cried out sharply in protest.

    _____

3. In our country murderers are no longer hung.

    _____

4. She said she will try to finish it in time.

    _____

5. My dog was took care of by my neighbour while I was away.

    _____

6. I borrowed him $900 to fix his car.

    _____

7. I brang back the wheel barrow when I had finished using it.

    _____

8. Despite the problems between I, we both went to the party.

    _____

9. I have copies of the cheques I had wrotten.

    _____

10. Do you want to come with?

    _____

11. You done good. Don't muck it up.

    _____

12. Has he showed you where to find the library?

    _____

Score: /24   Pass: 19/24

Section 2, Test 9: Phrases & Clauses

A. Each sentence below contains either an <u>adverbial clause or an adjectival clause.</u> Write the clause on the line provided and say if it is an adjectival or adverbial clause. Write the verb or noun it modifies. (3 points)

1. Frank, whose grandfather was dead, marched in memory of him in the Anzac Day Parade.

   _____

2. Are those the shoes you want to buy?

   _____

3. When I delivered the newspaper, I saw Mrs Smith at the window.

   _____

4. Brian has a dog that is fourteen years old.

   _____

5. If the jacket is too big for you I can alter it.

   _____

6. Phone us when you arrive in town.

   _____

B. Each sentence contains either an adverbial or adjectival phrase. Identify it. Write it on the line provided and say if it is an adjectival or adverbial phrase. Write the verb or noun it modifies. (3 points)

1. We raced our bicycles across the playground.

   _____

2. The house on the corner is mine.

   _____

3. Your brother plays football better than my brother.

   _____

4. Mary and Krystal are reading in the car.

   _____

5. Many members of my family enjoy cycling.

   _____

Score: /33　　　　　　　　　　　　　　　　**Pass: 25/33**

© Valerie Marett
Coroneos Publications

Australian Homeschooling #566
Test Your English 8

Section 2, Test 10: Malapropisms

A malapropism is a ludicrous misuse of a word. Replace the malapropism in italics with the correct word from the box. (1 point each)

inured, sportsmanship, ingenious, vacated, endure, infuriated, contiguous, conflicting, forceps, paradox, exhorted, geography, iridescent

1. I would like to learn *geometry* so I can learn something about *contagious* countries.

   _____

   _____

2. Seats on the council had to be *vaccinated* every three years.

   _____

3. Our doctor is so hard up he could not buy new *biceps*.

   _____

4. A politicians must *endear* a great many interruptions at public meetings.

   _____

5. Mr Jones was not *manured* to interruptions and is still *infatuated* by the expression of any opinion *afflicting* with his own.

   _____

   _____

6. The coach *exhausted* the pupils to play fairly and deal with each other in the true spirit of *supportiveness*.

   _____

   _____

7. Her party dress was as *incandescent* as a rainbow.

   _____

8. A calculator is an *ingenuous* instrument for making calculations.

   _____

9. A *orthodox* is a seemingly absurd contradiction of a statement.

   _____

Score: /13　　　　　　　　　　　　　　Pass: 10/13

© Valerie Marett
Coroneos Publications

Australian Homeschooling #566
Test Your English 8

Section 2, Test 11: Clauses and Phrases

A. Each sentence below contains an underlined portion. Say whether the underlined portion is a clause or phrase. (1 point each)

1. The box <u>on the table</u> contains Jack's birthday present.

   _____

2. Do you know <u>what is in the box?</u>

   _____

3. The painter is a person <u>of great talent.</u>

   _____

4. We saw the old woman as <u>she climbed the stairs.</u>

   _____

5. If Perry calls <u>please tell him I am on my way.</u>

   _____

B. Read each sentence below. Identify the subordinate clause. (2 points)

1. When the bell rings we should get to class.

   _____

2. I feel much more responsible since I got a new dog.

   _____

3. When we arrive, we will set up the tent.

   _____

4. When James glued on a wing, he found he had lost a piece.

   _____

5. As he walked to the store, James thought about his Dad who was overseas.

   _____

6. On a cold day the dogs stayed in their kennel where it was warm.

   _____

Score: /17   **Pass: 14/17**

© Valerie Marett
Coroneos Publications

Australian Homeschooling #566
Test Your English 8

Section 2, Test 12: Sentences

A. Combine the two sentences in every question below to make a complex sentence. Make each sentence as concise as possible. (2 point each.)

1. The Mighty Butterflies won the championship. They are my sister's team.

   _____

2. Kylie threw the ball. It went into the bushes.

   _____

3. This week in class I wrote a poem. Also, I wrote a song. Then, I wrote a story.

   _____

4. The man fled the country. He was wanted by the police.

   _____

5. There is nothing better in winter time than a warm room. It is also good to have a hot drink. Then all you need is a good book.

   _____

6. The boy came from a disadvantaged background. He did well academically.

   _____

B. Rewrite the sentences adding the correct punctuation. (1 point each change. The number is shown in brackets)

1. The baseball game which started at five was a perfect way to end a summer evening   (3)

   _____

   _____

2. Its such a pity We won't be able to play unless the run stops soon (3)

   _____

3. Please come inside now Mother said Its getting dark   (8)

   _____

4. Since we are expecting crowds we plan to arrive early   (2)

   _____

Score: /28   **Pass: 21/28**

Section 2, Test 13: More Malapropisms

A malapropism is the misuse of a word in mistake for one resembling it. The underlined word in each sentence below is a malapropism. Rewrite the sentence using the correct word. (1 point each word)

1. After five days without food the boy was found in an **emancipated** condition.

   _____

   _____

2. The **funereal** will leave at 2.30 p.m. for the **internment** in the family vault.

   _____

   _____

3. Do not **exasperate** your brother's faults.

   _____

4. Are you **incinerating** that I am not telling the truth?

   _____

5. He bought the television, cash on **deliverance.**

   _____

6. We intend to spend our Christmas **vocation** on the Sunshine Coast.

   _____

7. Correct this **amphibious** statement.

   _____

8. Owing to his parents' income he was **illegible** for a scholarship.

   _____

9. We decided to sign the **partition.**

   _____

10. The brakes on a bike work by **fraction.**

   _____

Score: /11   Pass: 8/11

Section 2, Test 14: Noun Clauses

A. Write the noun clause under each sentence. (2 points each question)

1. I don't know who left the gift there.

   _____

2. Ask your tutor if this is the correct answer.

   _____

3. I don't understand why you did that.

   _____

4. She tells whoever will listen.

   _____

5. What he said made a lot of sense.

   _____

B. Change the questions to a noun clause. The first one is completed for you.
(2 points each question)

1. What time is it?
   I would like to know *what time it is.*

2. Why don't they like to go dancing?

   _____

3. What is the reason for his failure?

   _____

4. Who left open the car door?

   _____

C. Replace the underlined noun phrase with a noun clause.   (2 points)

1. No one can guess <u>the time of his arrival.</u>

   _____

2. The doctors expect <u>an improvement in his health</u>.

   _____

Score: /20   **Pass: 16/20**

Section 2, Test 15: Choosing Better Words

One word in each sentence is underlined. Below each sentence four words are given. Select the better word and rewrite the sentence. (1 point each)

1. The committee has made a decision <u>of great importance.</u>
   a. momentary   b. sudden   c. momentous   d. forceful

   _____

2. We remarked on Mary's <u>ineluctable</u> personality.
   a. charming   b. irresistible   c. unpleasant   d. irritating

   _____

3. The committees are going to <u>come together.</u>
   a. coalesce   b. combine   c. segregate   d. fuse

   _____

4. The boy told me a <u>fantastic</u> story.
   a. thrilling   b. breathtaking   c. fanciful   d. exaggerated

   _____

5. Annette admired the <u>row of columns.</u>
   a. architecture   b. portico   c. arch   d. colonnade

   _____

6. The <u>tumour</u> was very small.
   a. ganglion   b. swelling   c. pimple   d. mass

   _____

7. She concluded her speech with an <u>insincere</u> remark.
   a. uncertain   b. flippant   c. obscure   d. angry

   _____

8. Her report was <u>false</u>.
   a. fictional   b. imaginary   c. valid   d. fictitious

   _____

9. His demands were <u>excessive.</u>
   a. reasonable   b. exorbitant   c. limitless   d. preposterous

   _____

Score: /9

Pass: 7/9

Australian Homeschooling #566
Test Your English 8

Section 2, Test 16: Condensing Sentences

Condense and rewrite each of these sentences to the number of words shown in brackets. (3 points each)

1. The man, whose job it is to put glass in the window frame, started work without waiting a minute longer. (5)

   _____

2. In the middle of the fifteenth century, a gentleman whose name was Gutenberg, invented a system consisting of metal letters which could be arranged into any desired words and afterwards taken out to be rearranged for other words. (7)

   _____

3. We remember as the clock strikes eleven o'clock on the eleventh day of November the ending of the second World War. (11)

   _____

4. It is in all probability true that the greatest advantage a surgeon can possess is not elaborate instruments or medical knowledge, but a steady hand. Such steadiness is a great advantage. (8)

   _____

5. A strange dog that ran with a limp appeared on the scene, as if he had dropped from the clouds. (5)

   _____

6. He breathed his last in indigent circumstances, though in the not so distant past his secretary, baliff, gardener, chauffeur and housekeeper all thought he was possessed of half the wealth of a Rockefeller. (11)

   _____

7. His captors stuffed something in his mouth to prevent his calling out, and then proceeded on their itinerary. (7)

   _____

8. On no single occasion has Mr Peacock lost his temper, not even when a live chicken jumped out of his boiled egg. (6)

   _____

Score: /24   **Pass: 18/24**

© Valerie Marett
Coroneos Publications

Australian Homeschooling #566
Test Your English 8

Section 2, Test 17: Word Meanings

Choose a word from the box to fit each meaning below: (1 point each)

> monotonous, enumerate, scrupulous, avaricious, symptom, obscure,
> militant, contagious, garrulous, parapet, consequence, profile,
> complacent, inaudible, calamity, intangible, infectious, lament

1. showing uncritical satisfaction with oneself _____

2.. not made of a physical substance, not able
    to be touched _____

3. talkative _____

4. to mourn or make cries of grief _____

5. dull, tedious and repetitious _____

6. breast high wall to protect people _____

7. to count the number of or to name over _____

8, thorough and extremely attentive to detail _____

9. having an extreme greed for material gain _____

10. a cause or effect, typically one that is
    unpleasant _____

11. a great misfortune _____

12. that which indicates the existence of
    something else _____

13. not easily discovered or known about _____

14. favouring confrontational or violent methods
    in support of a cause _____

15. unable to be heard _____

16. able to spread and infect another _____

17. side view of the head _____

Score: /17   **Pass: 14/17**

© Valerie Marett
Coroneos Publications

Australian Homeschooling #566
Test Your English 8

Section 2, Test 18: Complex Sentences.

A. Combine each group of sentences into a compound or complex sentence.
(1 point each)

1. The train approached the station. The two trains met.

   _____

2. We noticed several houses. Nobody was living in them.

   _____

3. The morning sky was overcast. It was threatening.

   _____

B. Use a conjunction to make a complex sentence. (1 point each)

1. He is not sure. He will be able to come.

   _____

2. Shall we see a picture? Shall we go out to dinner?

   _____

3. I cleaned the whole house. Mary did not help me.

   _____

C. Build a complex sentence by adding phrases or clauses. (2 points each)

1. He was shipwrecked on an island...............

   _____

2. I took a blank sheet of paper..................

   _____

3. .... when he saw the damage.......................

   _____

4. It is common knowledge...........................

   _____

5. .... that I may be late..............

   _____

Score: /16   **Pass: 13/16**

Section 2, Test 19: Colons

Rewrite the sentences using a colon correctly. (1 point each)

1. I have three hobbies. I collect coins, I write and I knit.

    _____

2. To Whom It May Concern

    _____

3. I have been really sad today. My cat, Fluffy, died.

    _____

4. I never go to bed until ten p.m.

    _____

5. I would like to visit the following places Italy, France and Brazil.

    _____

Semi-Colons

Rewrite the sentences using a colon and or semi-colon correctly.
(1 point each unless marked)

1. The house was ready. It was clean, the table set and the candles lit.

    _____

2. I said it would rain today. It seems I wasn't far wrong.

    _____

3. You will find references to herb gardens on pages 4, 38 and 43, to wild herbs on pages 18, 37 and 42.

    _____

    _____

4. Important nutrient groups include milk, butter and cheese, meat, poultry and eggs, green or yellow vegetables, cereals. (4 points)

    _____

    _____

5. He was the eldest son, consequently he inherited the title.

    _____

Score: /13   **Pass: 10/13**

Section 2, Test 20: Match the Words

Match the words in the box with the definitions. (1 point each.)

> sedate, impecunious, divulge, elicit, discretion, replenish, docile, pervade, frivolous, culprit

1. diffuse or extend through   _____

2. disclose, reveal   _____

3. ready to accept control or instruction   _____

4. the cause of a problem, guilty person   _____

5. calm, dignified, unhurried   _____

6. restore to a former level, fill up again   _____

7. not having any serious purpose or value   _____

8. having little or no money   _____

9. evoke or draw out   _____

10. freedom to decide what to do in a
    particular situation   _____

Change to Verbs

Change the following words to verbs. (1 point each.)

1. industrial   _____   2. indulgent   _____

3. humility   _____   4. prosperous   _____

5. pervasive   _____   6. deceptive   _____

Change to Adverbs

Change the following words to adverbs. (1 point each.)

1. conscious   _____   2. deceive   _____

3. pervade   _____   4. similarity   _____

Score: /20   Pass: 16/20

Section 2, Test 21: Adverbial Clauses

Adverbial clauses may be clauses of manner, time, place, reason, condition, concession, comparison, purpose or result.

Each underlined clause is an adverbial clause. State what kind of an adverbial clause it is, and name the word or words it modifies.

1. Move down a step please **so as I may see what is happening.** (2 pt)

   _____

2. **As he emerged** from the cave he looked so white **that we were shocked.** (4 pt)

   _____

   _____

3. There was something odd about the way they danced **although they seemed to move with surprising freedom and lightness.** (2 pt)

   _____

4. The mansion John built **was as large as three ordinary houses.** (2 pts)

   _____

5. **If Joel calls** please tell him I am on my way. (2 points)

   _____

6. We played on the beach **until the sun set.** (2 points)

   _____

7. On a cold day the dogs stayed in their kennel **where it was warm.** (2 pts)

   _____

8. Will you move you car please **so that I can get out?** (2 pts)

   _____

9. The light was shining so brilliantly **that you could not miss it.** (2 pts)

   _____

10. Tigers are generally regarded as being more ferocious **than lions.** (2 pts)

    _____

Score: /22   Pass: 18/22

Section 2, Test 22: Understanding Shakespeare

Answer these questions:

1. State the groups Shakespeare's plays can be divided into and give an example of each. (8 points)

   _____

   _____

2. List the common features in Shakespeare's tragedies. (6 points)

   _____

   _____

   _____

   _____

   _____

   _____

3. List the common features in Shakespeare's comedies. (9 points)

   _____

   _____

   _____

   _____

   _____

   _____

   _____

   _____

   _____

   _____

4. List the common features in Shakespeare's histories. (4 points)

   _____

   _____

   _____

   _____

5. Express the following in modern English. (1 point each)

   a. perchance _____   b. pray/prithee _____

Score: /29   **Pass: 23/29**

© Valerie Marett
Coroneos Publications

Australian Homeschooling #566
Test Your English 8

Section 2, Test 23: Noun Equivalents

Complete the sentence using the type of noun equivalent asked for in the bracket. (1 point each question)

1. The .... are always sad. (adjective)

   _____

2. .... good music is my favourite pastime. (gerund)

   _____

3. .... quiet for long is often too hard. (noun-infinitive)

   _____

4. Do you know .... rats there are? (noun phrase)

   _____

5. .... puzzled the scientists. (noun clause)

   _____

6. .... is an Australian summer activity. (gerund)

   _____

7. The .... are always with us. (adjective)

   _____

8. .... is up to you to decide. (noun clause)

   _____

9. .... we could not understand. (noun clause)

   _____

10. .... ran all the way home. (pronoun)

   _____

11. I want .... right up to the top. (noun-infinitive)

   _____

12. Realising .... we turned away. (noun clause)

   _____

Score: /12   **Pass: 8/12**

Section 2, Test 24: Find the Word

Rewrite the sentence, replacing the underlined word with a word from the box that has similar meaning. (1 point each word)

> reciprocate, inclement, solace, eschew, eccentric, fastidious, demeanour, vexation, ominous, allegiance, ostentatious, belligerent

1. The cricketer's **outward behaviour** irritated the spectators.

   _____

2. The building was a simple design without being **pretentious.**

   _____

3. The priest gave the dying man **comfort.**

   _____

4. The talkative student was responsible for the teacher's **annoyance.**

   _____

5. Doctors advise it is important to **avoid** smoking.

   _____

6. **Threatening clouds** were an indication of **bad** weather.

   _____

7. The cook was **hard to please** about cleanliness.

   _____

8. The accident victim was drunk and **ready to fight.**

   _____

9. The man was **unconventional and with slightly strange behaviour.**

   _____

10. The soldiers pledged their **loyalty** to the king.

    _____

11. Never **repay** evil with evil.

    _____

Score: /12   Pass: 9/12

© Valerie Marett
Coroneos Publications

Australian Homeschooling #566
Test Your English 8

Answers Test Your English 8

Section 1

Page 3 Test 1

A. Neuter Gender
Parent to check.
Examples: house, grass, lake, pen

B. Common Gender
Any order
people, poultry, children, sheep
you, we, us, they, them

C. Collective Nouns
1. board
2. horde
3. mob
4. pack/ deck
5. flight
6. swarm

D. Abstract Noun
1. superiority
2. sincerity
3. punctuality
4. patience

E. Noun of small quantity
1. speck
2. blade
3. splinter
4. slice
5. drop
6. lock/ strand

F. Replace underlined words
pessimist

Page 4 Test 2

A. Noun Plurals
1. calves
2. cherries
3. volcanoes
4. already plural—only the plural exists
5. mothers-in-law
6. antennae— unchanged
7. classes
8. termini
9. loaves
10. victories
11. handkerchiefs
12. delays
13. halves
14. lice
15. patches
16. legislation (unchanging)
17. vertebrae
18. bacilli
19. analyses
20. criteria
21. luggage (unchanging)
22. passers-by

B. Complete Sentence

1. Please buy me six tomatoes while you are out.
2. It has been bitterly cold and our area is experiencing a plague of mice.
3. There are few oases in the Nafud Desert.
4. I have had several different secretaries this year.
5. There are many pupae (or pupas) in my garden waiting until spring to hatch.

Page 5 Test 3

A. Correct Meaning
1. stationery
2. ingenious
3. contemptible
4. affect
5. mien

B. Add —ary or —ery

1. flattery	secondary
2. necessary	dromedary
apothecary	proprietary

C. —cy, or —sy
1. heresy
2. occupancy
3. ecstasy

D. —efy, or —ify
1. verify
2. putrefy

E. —ceed, —cede or —sede
1. accede
2. supersede
3. exceed
4. proceed
5. recede
6. succeed

Page 7 Test 4
Comprehension

A. Answer these questions:

1. The peace lasted 207 years. (From the accession of Augustus in 27 B.C. until the death of Marcus Aurellius in 180 A.D.)

2. It extended from Britain to Germany, all the way down to Spain and then right around the Mediterranean to the top of Africa.

3. Rome built roads and established forts.

4. The main purpose of the roads was to allow the army to get from one end of the Empire to the other very quickly and to keep Rome informed of developments and allow commands from Rome to be transmitted

to be quickly transmitted back.

5. Trade was able to get easily from the provinces to Rome.

6. Answer will vary slightly. Should include:
—clothing—designed to protect head and body without impeding movement.
—shield—protected body and could lock together with other shields to form a protective wall
—pair of javelins—designed so they would break when pulled out of the enemy's shields or body.
—long slashing sword gave dangerous wounds
—dagger for close up work.

7. With the Army went engineers to plan camps and forts and design bridges and roads; doctors to cure the wounded; light troops on horses with slings or bows; artillery men with their catapults and carts with food supplies.

8. Yes the Army was well trained. Every man had his job and knew how important it was to keep his place in line with the right amount of space to use weapons, and how important it was to obey orders.

B. Word Knowledge

1. pugio
2. impeding
3. Pax Roma
4. volley

Page 8 Test 5
A. Verb and type
1. finished (finite past tense) went (finite past tense)
2. instructed (transitive)
3. is (past participle) swimming (infinitive)
4. shouted (intransitive)

B. Nouns and verbs
1. Dad my canoe Father's Day race (n) was paddling (v)
2. clown ring spectators delight (n) tumbled screamed (v)
3. schooner sea storm (n) did was raging (v)
4. you work I (n) do will let go swimming (v)
5. He dogs (n) roams go (v)
6. He Dawn Fraser Olympics years (n) met swam (v)

Page 9 Test 6

Foreign Words & Phrases
1. repertoire
2. a la mode
3. premiere
4. a la carte
5. facade
6. tete-a-tete
7. bon appetit
8. debut
9. nom de plume
10. vinaigrette
11. resume
12. au fait
13. sabotage
14. fait accompli
15. boutique

Page 10 Test 7
A. Classification of adjective and noun
1. which: interrogative   article (n)
2. third: numerical   applicant (n)
   my: possessive   brother (n)
3. every: distributive   test (n)
   those: demonstrative   pupils (n)
   this: demonstrative   exam (n)
4. huge: descriptive   rock (n)
   steep: descriptive   hill (n)
   (more is a comparative adjective but the student hasn't been asked to classify it.)

B. One adjective
1. The jungle proved impenetrable.
2. This is the first time the aquatic event has been performed.
3. The early settlers saw the Great Dividing Range as an insurmountable barrier.
4. It was an unprecedented event.
5. The visitor behaved in an unceremonious manner.

Page 11 Test 8
A. Figures of Speech
1. personification
2. alliteration
3. hyperbole
4. metaphor
5. simile
6. pun
7. alliteration, onomatopoeia
8. hyperbole

B. Similes in a Sentence
Parent to check.

C. Explain simile
Answers may vary slightly
1. to sleep soundly
2. very smart, up to all the tricks
3. to work very hard

Answers Test Your English 8

Page 12 Test 9
A. Adverb modifies verb, adjective or adverb
1. adjective
2. verb
3. adjective
4. adverb
5. verb
6. adjective
7. adverb
8. verb

B. Adverb of manner, time, place
1. again — time
2. here — place
3. noisily — manner
4. slowly — manner
5. outside — place
6. tomorrow — time
7. now — time
8. carefully — manner
9. here — place

Page 13 Test 10
1. petit four
2. au fait
3. piece de resistance
4. protégé
5. déjà vu
6. attaché
7. hors d'oeuvre
8. haute coutre
9. café au lait
10. faux pas
11. par excellence
12. cordon bleu
13. maître d'
14. en route
15. ensuite
16. matinee
17. potpourri

Page 14 Test 11
Figurative Expressions
1. to climb on the bandwagon
2. to keep someone at arm's length
3. to ring down the curtain
4. to pick someone's brains
5. a dog's breakfast
6. to play it by ear
7. caught red-handed
8. make no bones about it
9. to set one's teeth on edge
10. take a back seat
11. a kangaroo court
12. a red rag to a bull
13. on the ball
14. eat humble pie

Page 15 Test 12
Pronouns
1. little   indefinite
2. I personal;   ourselves   reflexive
3. I personal;   each   distributive
4. those   demonstrative
5. theirs, ours   possessive
6. everyone   indefinite
7. he, he personal
8. she personal;   herself   reflexive
9. what interrogative;   he, you personal
10. mine   possessive
11. something indefinite;   my   possessive
12. it   impersonal
13. this   demonstrative
14. who   relative
15. either   distributive
16. some, some   indefinite

Page 16 Test 13
Inserting proper nouns
1. China
2. January
3. Montreal
4. Pacific
5. Alexander Bell
6. Virgin
7. Mars
8. Robert Scott
9. Francis Drake
10. Holden
11. Endeavour
12. Mississippi
13. Tasmania
14. Mozart
15. Kosciusko
16. Mandarin
17. Christmas
18. Governor General
19. Victoria
20. Marie
21. Uluru
22. South America

Food Twins
1. chips
2. cream
3. tomato sauce
4. mint sauce
5. crackers
6. lemons
7. eggs
8. marmalade

Answers Test Your English 8

Page 17 Test 14
A. Prepositions
1. head—noun governed
   on the head—phrase
   him head—relationship
2. flag breeze—noun governed
   on the flag—phrase
   in the breeze—phrase
   eyes flag—relationship
   flag breeze—relationship
3. friend—noun governed
   to his friend—phrase
   salt friend—relationship
4. skirt—noun governed
   in the red skirt—phrase
   girl skirt—relationship

B. Correct Preposition
1. to   about
2. upon
3. on
4. among
5. to
6. with
7. against   for (any order)
8. with

Page 18 Test 15
Ambiguity
1. Lord Byron was born in this room with the strange key hole.
2. In my mind I have a picture of the place where we saw all the rubbish.
3. To Rent: Neat, well-kept townhouse, presently occupied by the owner, with two bedrooms and spacious bathroom.
4. Climbing a hill they saw a creek flowing below them.
5. She was surprised, while putting on her lipstick, by Mr Stephen's arrival.
6. The farmer wanted a man to keep his accounts and look after his cow.
7. While skipping down the hill he was run over by a car.
8. We have all read your book and many have enjoyed it.
9. Sitting in the car he watched the approach of the storm.
10. We found the dog called Spot who belonged to the lady (who lived next door.)

Page 19 Test 16
A. Use conjunction to complete sentence
1. Shall we go swimming or shall we play tennis?
2. Ian won the race though he was not considered a good runner.
3. He is not sure that he will be able to come.
4. I looked for it even though John would not help me.
5. He opened his book and read a chapter.
6. We held the oars as we had been instructed.

B. Underline conjunction
1. wherever
2. in order to
3. whenever
4. so that
5. although

C. Add a conjunction
1. and
2. As it (do not start with because)

Page 20 Test 17
(1 point for type of sentence. 1 point for function of that sentence.)
1. command intended to solicit a direct action
2. greeting
3. statement communicating an inference
4. rhetorical question
5. response indicating the listener is paying attention
6. response to conventional greeting
7. statement communicating an observation
8. question intended to illicit a direct answer
9. response not in the form of a normal statement
10. question expressing doubt
11. statement communicating judgement

Page 21 Test 18
Correct Word
1. casual
2. corroborated
3. eventuated
4. economical
5. excluded
6. idyll
7. causal
8. latter
9. libel
10. location
11. masterly
12. loath
13. oblivious
14. reign

Page 22 Test 19
Important Terms
1. fable

Answers Test Your English 8

2. alliteration
3. irony
4. couplet
5. epitaph
6. epigram
7. cliché
8. anticlimax
9. spoonerism
10. antithesis

Page 23 Test 20
1. she—subject
   drank a bottle of water—predicate
   water—object
2. oxygen—subject
   is essential for life on earth—predicate
   life—object
3. Children—subject
   behave badly—predicate
   Children (understood)—subject
   create problems—predicate
   problems—object
4. His sister—subject
   mended them with great skill—predicate
   them—object
5. you (understood)—subject
   be careful—predicate
   the dog—subject
   might bite you—predicate
   you—object
6. We—subject
   ate a hamburger at Hungry Jack's—predicate
   hamburger—object
7. Dad—subject
   bought his son a new coat—predicate
   son (direct object) coat (indirect object)
8. Everyone—subject
   brought food today—predicate
   food—object
9. Roger—subject
   lent Stephen his camera—predicate
   Stephen—direct object
   camera—indirect object
10. We—subject
    saw and **touched** the baby koala—predicate
    koala—object

Page 24 Test 21
1. credible
2. emetics
3. equivocal
4. auspicious
5. bracing
6. amphibious

7. monogamy
8. geography   contiguous
9. infuriated
10. inured
11. electrocutions   inexperience
12. endure   vociferous

Page 25 Test 22
1. Main clause: Gordon forgot his sunscreen
   Subordinate clause: even though he knew he burnt easily
2. Main clause: the engine was smoking
   Subordinate clause: when the airplane landed
3. Main clause: Max went shopping
   Subordinate clause: and (Max) bought some books that were on sale.
4. Main clause: John caught some fish
   Subordinate clause: After Kelly caught one also
5. Main clause: I like to eat lunch outside
   Subordinate clause: when the sun is shining
6. Main clause: The ball bounced on to the roof
   Subordinate clause: where Casey and Robert can not reach it.
7. Main clause: Tom plays many sports
   Subordinate clause: although he likes playing tennis best.

Page 26 Test 23
1. He acted irresponsibly.
2. The judge could not exonerate the accused.
3. At last he was able to convince the pessimists there was hope.
4. Lost on their hike, the scouts no longer regarded their leader as infallible.
5. Rabbits were at one time ubiquitous in Australia.
6. My brother is ambidextrous.
7. The company prescribed fixed hours for its employees.
8. The accident left him with a conspicuous scar on his face.
9. Rhetoric is often used unscrupulously.
10. Procrastination is the thief of time.

Page 27 Test 24
Latin Prefixes
1. posthumous
2. recant
3. recapitulate
4. subvert

Answers Test Your English 8

3. recapitulate
4. subvert
5. unison
6. redound
7. benevolent
8. conjunction
9. disinter
10. exculpate
11. interpose
12. preposterous
13. procrastinate
14. supersede
15. unanimous
16. procure

Page 28 Test 25
A. Change simile to metaphor
1. Geology is a closed book to me.
2. You must take the bull by the horns.
3. You are putting the cart before the horse.

B. Personification, hyperbole, pun, epigram, onomatopoeia, alliteration, metaphor or simile?
1. pun
2. alliteration
3. hyperbole
4. metaphor
5. personification
6. epigram
7. onomatopoeia
8. simile
9. personification
10. onomatopoeia

Page 29 Test 26
A. Adjectival clause & noun modified
1. for whom I made this cake (adj. clause)
   friend (noun)
2. who selected the best class song (adj. clause)
   student (noun)
3. (that) you bought—that is implied (adj. clause)
   that (pronoun)
4. which they handled very well (adj. clause)
   duties (noun)
5. who called this morning (adj. clause)
   customer (noun)

B. Adjectival and main clause
1. which you are moving to (adj. clause)
   tell me about the place (main clause)
2. whose name is well known (adj clause)
   he is an author (main clause)

3. whom they named (adj. clause)
   the man is a noted explorer (main clause)
4. who advocated the union of the Australian colonies (adj. clause)
   Henry Parkes was one of those men (main clause)
5. that he has not travelled (adj. clause)
   there are few lands (main clause)
6. where you are going (adj. clause)
   tell me about the place (main clause)

Answers Test Your English 8

Section 2

Page 31, Test 1
Better Words

A. One word for many
1. The king showed great magnanimity in dealing with the rebels.
2. The jury found it difficult to come to a decision.
3. The train approached the junction.
4. Who would win the Grand Final this year was a subject for speculation.
5. My friend is a pessimist.

B. Replace with a synonym
1. ultimately   attain
2. disorder   catastrophe   incredible
3. authentic   forged
4. understanding   obstinate   attempt remedy

Page 32, Test 2
Principal & Subordinate Clause

1. **Principal clause:** All the books have already been borrowed.
   Subordinate clause: which sounded really interesting

2. **Principal clause:** I am looking forward to the moment
   Subordinate clause: when I finish this course

3. **Principal clause:** There is a man at the door.
   Subordinate clause: who wants to see you

4. **Principal clause:** Do you remember the name of the man?
   Subordinate clause: whom you met yesterday

5. **Principal clause:** The man is a professional tennis player.
   Subordinate clause: whose wife teaches English

6. **Principal clause:** Can you remember the exact spot?
   Subordinate clause: that you dropped it

7. **Principal clause:** It is an ill wind
   Subordinate clause: that blows nobody any good

8. **Principal clause:** None of those people were known to us.
   Subordinate clause: whom he mentioned

Page 33, Test 3

Correct Useage

A. Choose the correct verb
1. Hunger and thirst are the cause of much human suffering.
2. Surely each of these men has been told to come prepared for this trial.
3. Australia in cultivating and harvesting is highly mechanised.
4. Every one of the boys has finished their homework.

B. Correct the sentence
1. It was me who you saw near the gate in the lane.
2. Whose overnight bag was beside the hedge?
3. Jane said that she and I were the best cooks in the class.
4. Always purchase Cadbury's chocolate as they are the best on the market.
5. We were not surprised at the result, but now we must prepare a new plan.

Page 35, Test 4
Poetry

A. Answer these questions:
1. The theme is the beauty and range of colours found in the world around her.
2. The poem is a descriptive poem written in eight verses (stanzas) and the second and fourth line of the poem rhyme.
3. Answers will vary. Answer should include: Each verse changes the scene and this presents constant contrasting landscape and times. For example, verse 2 where the author speaks of the sunset and verse 3 where she contrasts this with night. Then in verse 4 she speaks of the types and colours of the rocks to then return to verse 5 to the plains and the flowers covering them.
4. simile: yellow as sunburnt wheat
   metaphor: a wide purple sea
   onomatopoeia: creams and hisses
5. The Darling pea is a pretty weed that thrives after bushfires and kills cattle because of its addictive nature. This is why she calls it evil.
   she calls it evil.
5.

Answers Test Your English 8

6. Answers will vary: should include the continuous use of adjectives to give the reader a more in depth picture and enables the reader to share the poet's wonder and enjoyment of the colours around her.

7. Her main thought is that colour has seeped so deeply into her mind that even if she lost her sight she would remember the many varied colours of the world around her.

Page 36, Test 5
A. Adjectival Clauses

1. where we will leave the train (clause)
   station (noun)

2. when I finish work (clause)
   moment (noun)

3. whose daughter is going to marry Tony (clause)   John (noun)

4. who wants to see you (clause)
   man (noun)

5. who called a few minutes ago (clause)
   Peter (noun)

6. which sounded interesting (clause)
   books (noun)

B. Adjectival Phrases

1. although a clever boy (phrase)
   Andrew (noun)

2. in the cot (phrase)
   baby (noun)

3. near its mother (phrase)
   calf (noun)

   of the car (phrase)
   (the) backfire (noun)

4. on the table (phrase)
   book (noun)

Page 37, Test 6
A. Collective nouns
1. range
2. ream
3. flock
4. cavalcade
5. orchestra
6. bench
7. bed
8. mob
9. coalition
10. litter
11. squabble

12. band

B. Plurals
1. infernos
2. ratios
3. sheep
4. storeys
5. memoranda
6. diagnoses
7. cities
8. dingoes
9. halves
10. knives
11. species
12. wharves
13. bureaux
14. criteria

C. Correct Word
1. legible
2. allusion
3. complement
4. abhorent
5. precede
6. ingenious

Page 38, Test 7
A. Adverbial Phrases

1. in the morning (phrase)
   shaves (verb)   when

2. with great skill (phrase)
   mended (verb)   how

3. underneath the old bucket (phrase)
   found (verb)   where

4. in spite of the rain (phrase)
   enjoyed (verb)   when

5. for his raincoat (phrase)
   ran (verb)   why

   inside the house (phrase)
   ran (verb)   where

B. Adverbial Clause

1. as it was too wet (clause)
   played (verb)   reason

2. when the water sprayed him (clause)
   shivered (verb)   time

3. as our teacher had shown us (clause)
   practised (verb)   manner

4. where the hole had already been dug (clause)
   planted (verb)   place

© Valerie Marett
Coroneos Publications

Australian Homeschooling #566
Test Your English 8

5. as his leg hurt (clause)
   hurry (verb)   reason

6. to avoid being hurt (clause)
   jumped (verb)   reason

   when I saw the cyclist (clause)
   jumped (verb)   time

7. as the diagram shows (clause)
   turn (verb)   manner

Page 39, Test 8
Correct Sentences

1. Mr Jones finished his work and went home.

2. Surprised, he cried out in protest.

3. In our country murderers are no longer hanged.

4. She said she would try to finish it in time.

5. My dog was taken care of by my neighbour while I was away.

6. I lent him $900 to fix his car.

7. I brought back the wheelbarrow when I had finished using it.

8. Despite the problems between us, we both went to the party.

9. I have copies of the cheques I have written.

10. Do you want to come with me?

11. You have done well. Don't spoil it.

12. Has he shown you where to find the library?

Page 40, Test 9
A. Adverbial or Adjectival Clauses

1. whose grandfather was dead
   (adjectival clause)
   Frank (noun)

2. you want to buy (adjectival clause)
   shoes (noun)

3. when I delivered the newspaper
   (adverbial clause) saw (verb)

4. that is fourteen years old
   (adjectival clause) has (verb)

5. if the jacket is too big for you
   (adverbial clause) alter (verb)

6. when you arrive in town
   (adverbial clause) phone (verb)

B. Adverbial or Adjectival Phrase

1. across the playground (adverbial phrase) raced (verb)

2. on the corner (adjectival phrase) the house (noun)

3. better than my brother (adverbial phrase)   plays (verb)

4. in the car (adverbial phrase) are reading (verb)

5. of my family (adjectival phrase) members (noun)

Page 41, Test 10
Malapropisms

1. geography   contiguous
2. vacated
3. forceps
4. endure
5. inured   infuriated   conflicting
6. exhorted   sportsmanship
7. iridescent
8. ingenious
9. paradox

Page 42, Test 11
A. Clause or Phrase

1. phrase
2. clause
3. phrase
4. clause
5. clause

B. Subordinate clause

1. the bell rings

2. I got a new dog

3. we arrive

4. James glued on a wing

5. James thought about his Dad

6. it was warm

Page 43, Test 12
Sentences

A. Complex sentences

1. The Mighty Butterflies, my sister's team, won the championship.

2. Kylie threw the ball into the bushes.

Answers Test Your English 8

3. This week in class I wrote a poem, a song and a story.

4. The man fled the country because he was wanted by the police.

5. There is nothing better in winter time than a warm room, a hot drink and a good book.

6. Although the boy came from a disadvantaged background, he did well academically.

B. Correct punctuation

1. The baseball game, which started at five, was the perfect way to end a summer evening.

2. It's such a pity! We won't be able to play unless the rain stops soon.

3. "Please come inside now," Mother said. "It's getting dark."

4. Since we are expecting crowds, we plan to arrive early.

Page 44, Test 13
More Malapropisms

1. After five days without food the boy was found in an emaciated condition.

2. The funeral will leave at 2.30pm for the interment in the family vault.

3. Do not exaggerate your brother's faults.

4. Are you insinuating that I am not telling the truth?

5. He bought the television, cash on delivery.

6. We intend to spend our Christmas vacation on the Sunshine Coast.

7. Correct this ambiguous statement.

8. Owing to his parents' income he was ineligible for a scholarship.

9. We decided to sign the petition.

10. The brakes on a bike work by friction.

Page 45, Test 14

A. Noun Clause

1. who left the gift there

2. if this is the correct answer

3. why you did that

4. whoever will listen

5. what he said

B. Change the question to a noun clause
(answer may vary slightly)

2. Why they don't like to go dancing is a mystery.

3. Nobody knows the reason for his failure.

4. He didn't see who left open the car door.

C. Replace the noun phrase with a noun clause

1. No one can guess when he will arrive.

2. The doctors expect that his health will improve.

Page 46, Test 15
Choosing Better Words

1. The committee has made a <u>momentous</u> decision.

2. We remarked on Mary's <u>irresistible</u> personality.

3. Both <u>combine</u> and <u>coalesce</u> are correct. Of the two combine is better.

4. The boy told me a <u>fanciful</u> story. (This word is often misused today.)

5. Annette admired the <u>colonnade</u>.

6. The <u>ganglion</u> was very small.

7. She concluded her speech with a <u>flippant</u> remark.

8. Her report was fictitious.

9. His demands were exorbitant.

Page 47, Test 16
Condense Sentences
(There may be a slight variation in wording.)

1. The glazier started work immediately.

2. Gutenberg, a German, invented the printing press.

3. On Armistice Day we remember the ending of World War II.

4. A surgeon's greatest advantage is a steady hand.

5. An unknown, limping dog appeared.

6. He died poor even though his staff had considered him wealthy.

7. His captors gagged him before robbing him.

8. Mr Peacock never loses his temper.

Page 48, Test 17
Word Meanings

1. complacent
2. intangible
3. garrulous
4. lament
5. monotonous
6. parapet
7. enumerate
8. scrupulous
9. avaricious
10. consequence
11. calamity
12. symptom
13. obscure
14. militant
15. inaudible
16. infectious
17. profile

Page 49, Test 18
A. Compound or complex sentence
Answers may vary.
1. As the trains approached the station they met. or
   Approaching the station, the two trains met.

2. We noticed several houses in which nobody was living.

3. The morning sky was overcast and threatening.

B. Use conjunction to make complex sentences.

1. He is not sure whether (if) he will be able to come.

2. Shall we see a picture or shall we go out to dinner?

3. I cleaned the whole house although Mary did not help me.

C. Complete with phrases or clauses
Answers may vary.

1. He was shipwrecked on an island on which no one lived.

2. I took a sheet of paper and quickly wrote a receipt.

3. It was later that day when he saw the damage that the storm had caused.

4. It is common knowledge that the Southern Cross can be found on our flag.

5. It is possible that I may be late as the trains are not running because of the strike.

Page 50, Test 19
Colons

1. I have three hobbies: I collect coins, I read and I knit.

2. To Whom It May Concern:

3. I have been really sad today: my cat, Fluffy, died.

4. I never go to bed until 10:00 p.m.

5. I would like to visit the following places: Italy, France and Brazil.

Colons and Semi-colons

1. The house was ready: it was clean, the table was set and the candles lit.

2. I said it would rain today; it seems I wasn't far wrong.

3. You will find references to herb gardens on pages 4, 38 and 43; to wild herbs on pages 18, 37 and 42.

4. Important nutrient groups include: milk, butter and cheese; meat, poultry and eggs; green or yellow vegetables; cereals.

5. He was the eldest son; consequently he inherited the title.

Page 51, Test 20
Match the words

1. pervade
2. divulge
3. docile
4. culprit
5. sedate
6. replenish
7. frivolous
8. impecunious
9. elicit
10. discretion

Change to Verbs
1. industrialise
2. indulge
3. humiliate
4. prosper
5. pervade

6. deceive

Change to Adverbs
1. consciously
2. deceitfully
3. pervasively
4. similarly

Page 52, Test 21
Adverbial Clauses

1. adverbial clause of result
   <u>so as</u> modifies <u>see</u>

2. adverbial clause of time
   <u>as</u> modifies <u>emerged</u>
   adverbial clause of condition
   <u>that</u> modifies <u>shocked</u>

3. adverbial clause of condition
   <u>although</u> modifies <u>seemed</u>

4. adverbial clause of comparison
   <u>as</u> modifies <u>was</u>

5. adverbial clause of condition
   <u>if</u> modifies <u>calls</u>

6. adverbial clause of time
   <u>until</u> modifies <u>set</u>

7. adverbial clause of place
   <u>where</u> modifies <u>was</u>

8. adverbial clause of purpose
   <u>so</u> that modifies <u>can get</u>

9. adverbial clause of result
   <u>that</u> modifies <u>could not miss</u>

10. adverbial clause of comparison or
    degree
    <u>than</u> modifies <u>are</u> (understood)

Page 53, Test 22
Understanding Shakespeare

1. comedies, histories, tragedies,
   romances. Any of these:
   Comedies : The Merchant of Venice,
   Much Ado About Nothing,
   Midsummer Night's Dream
   The Taming of the Shrew, Twelfth Night
   Tragedies: Anthony and Cleopatra
   Hamlet, Julius Caesar, King Lear
   Macbeth, Othello, Romeo and Juliet
   Histories: Richard II, Richard III,
   Henry IV part 1 and 2, Henry V,
   Henry VI part 1, 2 and 3
   Romances: The Winter's Tale
   The Tempest, Cymbeline, Pericles
2. a tragic flaw

supernatural elements
internal or external conflict
fate or fortune
the theme of foul and revenge
paradox of life

3. a struggle for lovers to overcome
   problems
   the plot
   themes of love and friendship
   discord and resolution
   hero
   number of acts
   characters
   language
   ethical principles

4. focus on English monarchs
   not historically accurate
   explores the social structure of the
   time
   represents the compromise of life

5. a. perhaps
   b. please

Page 54, Test 23
Noun Equivalents
Answers may vary, suggestions below.

1. The <u>miserable</u> are always sad.

2. <u>Playing</u> good music is my favourite
   pastime.

3. <u>To keep</u> quiet is often too hard.

4. Do you know <u>how many</u> rats there
   are?

5. <u>Why Uranus rotated differently</u> puzzled
   the scientists.

6. <u>Surfing</u> is an Australian summer
   activity.

7. <u>The Poor</u> are always with us.

8. <u>What to bring</u> is up to you to decide.

9. <u>Why she was crying</u> we could not
   understand.

10. <u>He</u> ran all the way home.

11. I want <u>to climb</u> right up to the top.

12. Realising <u>everything was destroyed in
    the blaze</u> we turned away.

Page 55, Test 24
Find the Word
1. demeanour
2. ostentatious

Answers Test Your English 8

3. solace
4. vexation
5. eschew
6. ominous   inclement
7. fastidious
8. belligerent
9. eccentric
10. allegiance
11. reciprocate